The Old Things

Diana Noonan

Gran was moving to a small house.
She could not take all her old things.

Gran sent an e-mail to Tom.
She wanted to give him her old things.

To Tom ✖

From Gran Send

Dear Tom,

This is my record player.

It is very old!

I played music on it.

Would you like it?

Love,

Gran

To Gran
From Tom

Send

Dear Gran,

I play music on my MP3 player.

I would like your record player too.

Thank you.

Love,

Tom

P.S. Do you have some
records to play on it?

To **Tom**

From **Gran**

Send ✕

Dear Tom,
This is my old camera.
You will need film to take
a photo with it.
Would you like it?
Love,
Gran

To **Gran**

From **Tom**

Send

Dear Gran,
Thank you, but we have
a camera.
It shows a photo
as soon as you take it.
Bye,
Tom

Send

Dear Tom,

This is my typewriter.

It is very old!

I typed letters on it.

Would you like it?

Love,

Gran

For Tom!

To Gran ✖

From Tom Send

Dear Gran,

I type on Mom's laptop.

But it would be fun to type

on your typewriter.

Thank you.

Bye,

Tom

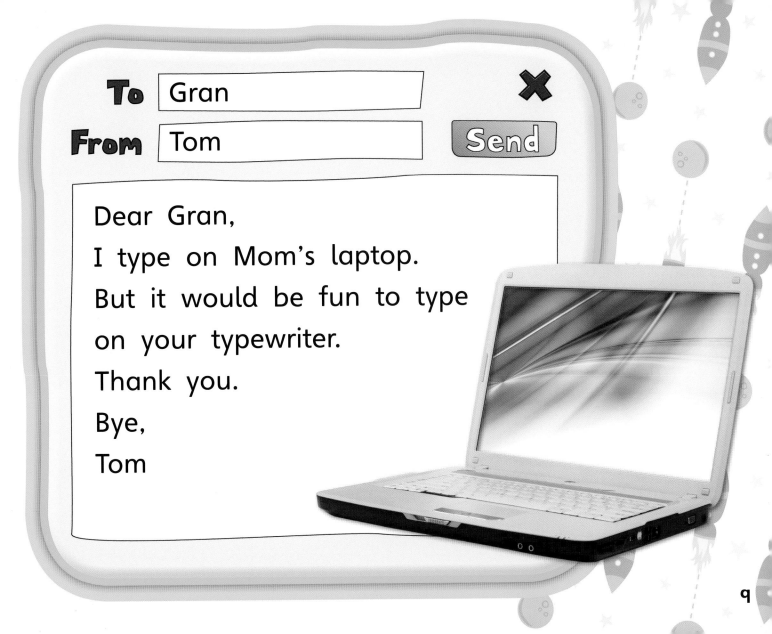

To Tom

From Gran

Send

Dear Tom,

This is my dad's telephone.

It is very old!

Would you like it?

Love,

Gran

To Gran

From Tom

S

Dear Gran,

Thank you, but I cannot use your old phone!

But I can call you on Dad's cell phone.

Love,

Tom

P.S. Dad's cell phone is so small!

To Tom

From Gran

Send

Dear Tom,

Here are my old pen and ink pot.

I used them at school.

I want to give them to you.

Love,

Gran

To Gran

From Tom

Send

Dear Gran,

Thank you for the pen and ink pot.

At school, I use these pencils.

Love,

Tom

P.S. How will you get
the old things
to my house?

To Tom

From Gran

Send

Dear Tom,

I will put the old things in a box.

I will mail them.

There was mail when I was a girl.

There is still mail now.

Some things stay the same!

Love,

Gran

Dear Gran,

Thank you for all the old things.

I will look after them!

Love,

Tom

P.S. The pen is fun to write with!

 record player   MP3 player

 camera   digital camera

 typewriter   laptop

 telephone   cell phone

 pen and ink   pencils